A SPIRIT DAUGHTER WORKBOOK

WRITTEN BY
JILL WINTERSTEEN

FOR THE LUNAR ECLIPSE

FRIDAY, MAY 5TH, 2023
10:34AM PT

THE LUNAR ECLIPSE

This May brings us the power of a lunar eclipse. Lunar eclipses are super-charged Full Moons that occur in conjunction with a solar eclipse. This eclipse continues the magic of the Aries solar eclipse that occurred on April 19th. It is also part of a set of seven eclipses taking place on the Taurus and Scorpio axis from November 2021 to October 2023.

Eclipses signify significant periods of change and transformation. These shifts do not take place all at once, though. They may start or continue on an eclipse, but their work continues throughout the period that eclipses are occurring in the same set of signs. Meaning, what occurs on this eclipse may be a continuation of events that occurred last fall or even last year at this time.

THE LUNAR ECLIPSE

While a solar eclipse opens the portal for new beginnings and change, a lunar eclipse reveals energies that help us complete a journey or shift our course in some way. Lunar eclipses are also much more emotionally charged compared to a solar eclipse, as they are more feminine in nature and affect the emotional body to a greater degree. They help us feel our intuition and honor the knowledge we hold. Sometimes we may not follow this knowledge, but it's always there, attempting to guide us.

A lunar eclipse is an opportunity to create significant change in your life. This change may come about abruptly, as lunar eclipses tend to bring information to you from out of the blue. You may find yourself feeling surprised or even caught off guard at some of the things you learn about others and yourself over a lunar eclipse. Not all of this information is negative. Some of it is positive and may even bring you inspiration, along with encouragement to shift your life.

Lunar eclipses, like Full Moons, are revealing. They reveal the truth in an often dramatic way and let you learn things that change your life course. It's important to accept what is revealed on a lunar eclipse. You cannot fight this knowledge, you can only take it in and ask yourself what is the highest manifestation you can create with this energy. Even if you are brought unwanted news or unexpected events, know that these are the Universe's way of giving you a life detour that will ultimately be the best course of action for your evolution. Open yourself up to the information available on an eclipse and trust that this is landing in your life at the exact moment you need it.

It's also important to understand that a lunar eclipse occurs to move you forward. It is an energetic push from the cosmos to take you out of stagnant energies and old patterns. Sometimes this forward motion can feel disruptive to your nervous system, and you may even resist it initially. There is no moving backward on the lunar eclipse, there is only a path forward. If you attempt to cling to energies that no longer serve your evolution, you will only be met with frustration and misalignment. If the lunar eclipse reveals something in your life that needs to be released, it's best to find the least dramatic way to move on.

The lunar eclipse and the month that follows it is an opportunity to detach from energies, emotions, and even people who do not serve your evolution. These changes can feel scary and uncomfortable, but once you cross the bridge to another way of being, you will feel as if you've broken through a wall built between you and your highest visions. Eclipses are the time to break through the barriers, in whatever form they take, that prevent you from reaching your potential. The emotional nature of a lunar eclipse often can cause an emotional breakdown as you break through these energies. Hold space for yourself and give yourself time to process the information revealed on the eclipse. Do not rush into any decisions at this time, but rather let the energy settle and then make whatever moves are needed to propel you forward.

Enjoy this eclipse and know that it is a special time in the year and in your life for you to make the changes needed to reach your energy and potential. Open yourself up to the information and energy available to you and know that the Universe is always here to support you and your journey. Trust your path and trust the path of this eclipse.

SCORPIO X LUNAR ECLIPSE

When the lunar eclipse meets Scorpio, magic is in the air. Scorpio is one of the most transformative signs of the zodiac. Paired with a lunar eclipse, this becomes a potent time for revelation, change, and immense psychological breakthroughs. The energy of the eclipse will affect everyone, and its energy will be intense. There will be no hiding from the vibrations this eclipse will bring everyone in the world. Through its intensity, this eclipse has the power to create any transformation you need in your life right now. It may not feel particularly good at the time it is occurring, but the change it creates ultimately opens the door for your highest energetic potential.

Ruled by water and the planet Pluto, Scorpio asks us to confront our deepest emotions. In doing so, Scorpio reminds us that we are magicians and healers. We can transform any energy, emotion, or behavior. We can turn darkness into light, and tension into relaxation. We can heal from the most painful wounds, turning them into wisdom, and we can navigate any storm with ease. The key in working with this energy is to be willing to feel. This eclipse asks us to put our logical mind at bay. It reminds us that when we analyze our feelings, we only prolong them. We need to feel to transform, and that means slowing down, courageously looking inward, crying, and holding space for any energy to rise from our subconscious.

SCORPIO X LUNAR ECLIPSE

What makes Scorpio's energy so intense is that it brings us face-to-face with the present moment. It asks us to stop in our tracks, let go of our distractions, and confront our inner reality. In the red glow of this eclipse, our facades are stripped away. This energy cuts through any exterior and brings us to the heart of the matter. We cannot lie to ourselves on this eclipse, and we cannot be lied to. It is a time of revelation, when our shadows come out to be seen in the full light of the Moon. Our unprocessed emotions come out to heal, our suppressed memories are triggered to awaken, and it is obvious how we project our wounds onto others. This revelation can cause many emotional reactions and may even make us feel as if we entered a downward spiral of negativity against ourselves. It's important to know that when shadows are revealed, it's best to accept them and understand them. It is through love, compassion, and acceptance that our shadows come out of the darkness and meet us in the light.

This eclipse is a potent time for shadow work and its resulting transformation. It all starts with the willingness to look beneath the surface of your conscious mind and become keenly aware of who you are. Transformation begins with confronting what is occurring right now. It may be challenging, uncomfortable, and downright nerve-wracking to take an honest look at your unconscious tendencies. Scorpio points out, though, that what is underneath the surface is still controlling you even if you don't acknowledge it. We are puppets, and our unconscious energies are the strings that pull us. When you face your deepest fears, triggers, beliefs, and conditioned patterns, you cut the strings and free yourself. You take control of your life and your behavior.

Facing the depths of your shadows and revealing the truth of your soul is the work of the Scorpio lunar eclipse. It's scary, intense, and full of raw emotions. It's also incredibly healing and empowering. This eclipse is here to remind you of your power. Facing your shadows takes courage and compassion. As you shift through your deeper layers this eclipse, remember to love all of them. They are all part of you and your story. They need love and acceptance to heal. As you discover hidden pieces of yourself, shine a light on them. Know that you are only human. You are not perfect—and that is ok. You are full of both darkness and light. The important part is that you learn about both sides of yourself. Only through knowing your whole self can you reach your highest potential.

Throughout this eclipse, pay attention to your feelings, intuition, and signs from the Universe. This energy will begin about two days before the eclipse and last for about two days after. If at any point in this window you have the urge to cry, do it. If you want to scream, do that too. If you need to hit a pillow with a bat for an hour, go for it. Follow your emotions without question. Just remember to be kind to others, as they are going through these intense energies as well. As feelings arise, sit with them and let them run through you. Journal to learn more. Ask yourself what you are feeling and what this feeling helps you understand about yourself. Avoid distractions, though. Notice your reactions and your triggers. Also notice when you feel surprised by a thought or a feeling. Remember, this eclipse just might show you something essential for your evolution, so pay attention. Give yourself time to process whatever is arising in your field and avoid making any hasty decisions at this time. This energy is part of a continuing path that will last throughout the year. Allow your transformation to unfold naturally. Be kind to yourself and know you are exactly where you need to be right now for your highest energetic evolution.

SCORPIO MOON X TAURUS SUN

While the Moon is in Scorpio, the Sun remains in Taurus, bringing us both of their energies to work with this Full Moon. Scorpio and Taurus stand in opposition in the sky and on the zodiac wheel. They both, though, ask us to do the same thing: ground our energy in the present moment. As we work with the power of Scorpio this eclipse, we also work with the power of Taurus. Every astrological energy has a low side and a high side. The eclipse offers us the opportunity to look at each side of the signs involved and determine how we might align with them. We can then release and shift our patterns, which embody lower frequencies and vibrate to a higher level.

Scorpio and Taurus both want us to become completely absorbed in the present moment. They ask us to set aside our anxiety about the future or pain of the past and feel the moment. Taurus encourages us to connect with Mother Nature and use our senses to find presence. In contrast, Scorpio asks us to connect with our inner world and release emotional reactions to find presence. Both of these signs ask us to align with the rhythms of the Universe—Taurus, by connecting with the Earth, and Scorpio by connecting with ourselves. Over this eclipse, we have the opportunity to feel one with everything around us and know that we are part of the magic in the Universe. We can feel how we are made of the same energy as the trees, the oceans, the mountains, and the stars. We can feel the vastness of life and become inspired by our own power.

While Scorpio and Taurus both connect us to the infinite rhythms of the Universe, they differ in their view of resources. Scorpio focuses on energetic resources, like time to transform, space to feel, and courage to travel inward. On the other hand, Taurus focuses on tangible assets, like a physical space to feel supported, external comforts to soothe, and food for the body. Both of these signs give us tools that help us ground our energy, transform what we need to through healing, and step into unknown territory. They both want us to feel our power and our oneness with everything in the Universe. They just each have a different method for getting us to this place.

This eclipse brings us great opportunities to do shadow work, which helps us understand how we limit ourselves out of fear and insecurity. Our shadow is where we store all of our unprocessed emotions, including those from childhood. It forms the basis of our unconscious reactions. It also represents our deeper wounds that forced us to store emotions that the conscious mind could not understand when they occurred. Our shadow works behind the scenes and often undermines our conscious efforts to manifest our dreams. We can begin to understand our shadows by looking at the lower frequencies of zodiac signs on the eclipse. They can help us understand how we may act on our shadows and bring light to unconscious patterns. Scorpio's and Taurus's low sides bring us away from our power and place it outside ourselves. The Scorpio eclipse allows us to look at our shadows around our self-worth, fear, inner reliance, and overall power.

When we align with the low side of Scorpio, we don't allow ourselves to feel. We distract ourselves with external preoccupations, which leads to anxiety and obsession. We also find clever ways to avoid the internal work we need to do to transform ourselves and our lives. We blame others, project our feelings onto them, and ignore our internal cries for help. Instead of facing our deepest fear, wounds, and pain with courage, we avoid these places in ourselves. We also mistrust our intuition and instead look outside ourselves for validation of our self-worth. We may obsess over money, loved ones, and our place in the world.

In this lower frequency of Scorpio, we avoid our true feelings, forgetting that they are a place of power and allowing them to control us subconsciously. They pull our strings and sabotage our intentions to build our visions. They can make us feel helpless. Instead of owning our power, we slip into a victim consciousness, where we feel everything is being done to us and we are helpless against it. This low, or shadow, side can make us feel we don't belong anywhere and are alone in this world. Without inner reliance on ourselves, we may feel we have no rock to stand on and that the ground will slip out from beneath us at any moment. We are then triggered when issues come up around security, revealing our shadow of feeling unsafe in the world.

We can also become stuck in a transformational loop, never accepting our perfection. We may also look for the next shift we need to make in our lives, never appreciating what we have already accomplished. This is the part of us that self-sabotages so we may build again, transform again, and do it better next time. Scorpio is the rising Phoenix, but sometimes the Phoenix does not need to rise. She just needs to fly.

Taurus holds a similar low side in regards to resources. When we align with the low side of Taurus, we also feel insecure. We may obsess over material possessions and finances, thinking they define us. We forget our ability to create abundance through inner reliance and creativity and instead seek it externally. We move away from stillness and peace only to become preoccupied with the figure in a bank account. We may even compete for resources, taking on a scarcity mindset and forgetting that abundance is everywhere. Taurus's low side is full of anxiety and thinking about future scenarios. Instead of staying in the moment, we go to the future in fear, thinking we might lose everything. We become triggered by others who appear successful, and we experience jealousy or envy. We forget that we can never lose our most valuable resource: ourselves.

The low sides of both signs are a question of security, worth, and underlying fear. When we align with Taurus's shadow side, we place all of our value on the goods we can collect. When we align with Scorpio's, we lose touch with our power and rely on others to tell us our worth, often continuously altering ourselves to meet their standards. Both low sides lack understanding of their oneness with nature, and both find it impossible to stay grounded in their power moment to moment. If you find yourself aligning with either of these low sides, know that is ok. You are seeing your shadows. It's challenging to become aware of your shadow sides, but it is essential if you are going to shift them. The first step in confronting these lower frequencies is to sit still and allow yourself to feel. You may cry, journal, laugh, or experience a roller coaster of emotions, but feeling is the way through. You must travel through the depths of your body and the stories that you live with each day. You may not want to read them, but they are always there. It's best to take control of them so they don't control you any longer.

In working with this eclipse, ask yourself if you have become preoccupied with things outside yourself as a means to distract you from what's within. Have you felt obsessed about resources and untrusting of your ability to create abundance? Have you looked to others for security instead of owning your power? Furthermore, have you forgotten your connection with the Universe? As you look at some of these lower aspects of Taurus and Scorpio in yourself, have compassion and courage. Release what you can this eclipse and know that just becoming aware of these energies is enough to be a catalyst for great transformation. It all starts, though, with your willingness to look deeply at yourself as you stay grounded in the present moment. Align with the Sun in Taurus to feel held by the Earth as you align with the Moon to feel into the deepest places of your soul. Enjoy the journey of learning about your whole self.

ASPECTS

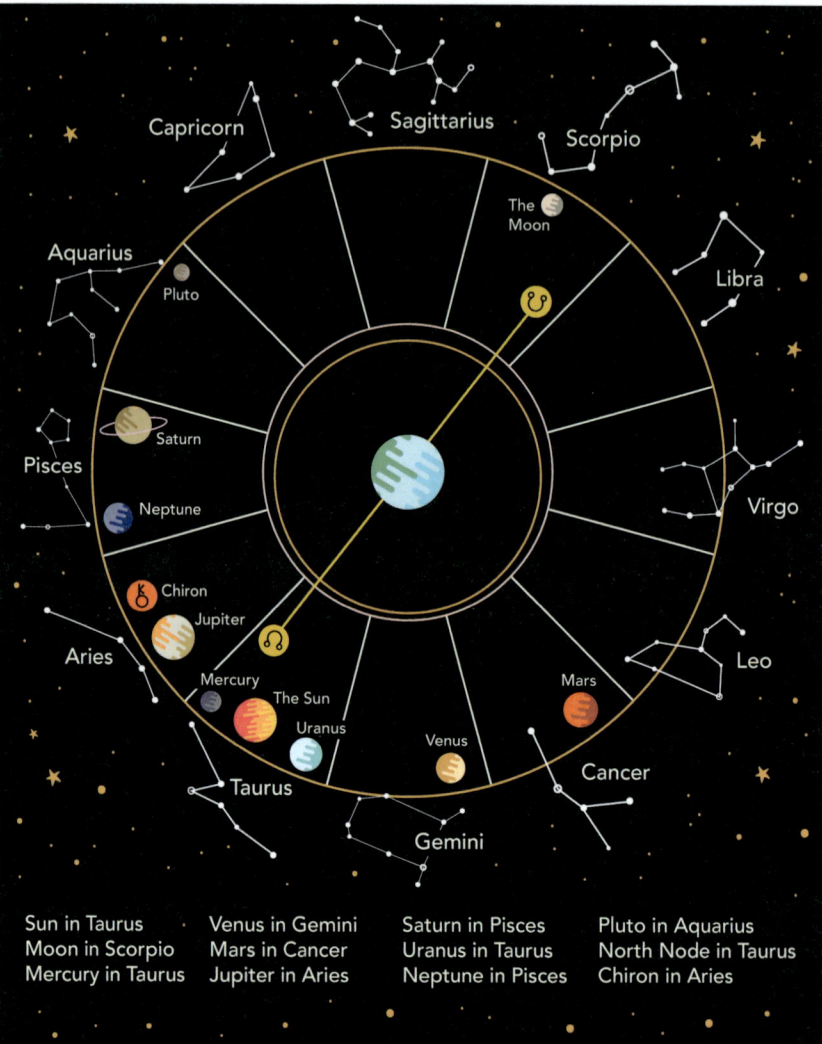

Sun in Taurus	Venus in Gemini	Saturn in Pisces	Pluto in Aquarius
Moon in Scorpio	Mars in Cancer	Uranus in Taurus	North Node in Taurus
Mercury in Taurus	Jupiter in Aries	Neptune in Pisces	Chiron in Aries

The Scorpio lunar eclipse takes place at 14° Scorpio, supercharging this point in the sky. If you would like to go deeper into understanding how this eclipse may affect you, look at your natal chart and see if you have any planets or cosmic bodies around this degree of Scorpio. Look around 14° Taurus directly opposite for planets or cosmic bodies. You can also look at the other fixed signs, Leo and Aquarius, to see if you have any planets around 14° in these signs. If you do happen to have planets in any of these positions, know that this eclipse will affect you more intensely than others. You may feel at odds with yourself and the world over this period. It ultimately will be an amazing time for transformative breakthroughs for you, although the journey may feel quite challenging. Ground your energy and find support from the people around you during this time. Know that whatever is happening is for the best. You are evolving at a great speed right now, and on the other side of this evolution is a new way of being.

ASPECTS

If you don't have planets in these positions, know that the eclipse will also affect you. It will affect everyone on the planet whether you can view it or not. Its energy will be intense and will open up portals of transformation for all beings. There are also some other aspects affecting this eclipse that everyone will feel. Aspects occur when other cosmic bodies form certain degrees with the Sun and Moon. Degrees of significance include 180, 150, 120, 90, 60, and 0. This is also how we look at our own planetary placements compared to the current Moon and Sun position. Is good to look at your natal chart to see if you have any planets that form these degrees of importance with the Moon. They will be at or around 14°. As mentioned, planets in fixed signs bring the most intensity, but planets in other signs can also impact how you feel on this eclipse. For instance, if you have planets in Water signs at these degrees, you find this eclipse brings beneficial energy to your life and feelings of ease. It may heighten your intuition or give you heightened insights into your life.

In looking at the current sky on this eclipse, we see that Moon opposes Mercury and Uranus, also in Taurus. The Moon also forms a trine, or 120° aspect with Mars in Cancer. The Sun forms a sextile, or 60° aspect with Mars. Trine and sextile aspects are beneficial influences. They add their power to the eclipse, heightening and harmonizing with the already existing energies.

With Uranus and Mercury involved in this Eclipse, we are encouraged to have conversations with ourselves and others about breakthroughs that are needed in our lives. Uranus helps us unravel and reveal old patterns. Through this revelation, we can change. Uranus, though, often helps us see the truth through shocking experiences that can somewhat rattle our nervous system. Be open to information coming your way this Eclipse that breaks you free of old patterns no longer serving you. These downloads may feel overwhelming at first but will ultimately change the trajectory of your behavior, actions, emotion, and life. This Eclipse is somewhat of a repeat of the energy available that May when the Lunar Eclipse occurred in Scorpio. Much of the vibrations are the same. Consider it another opportunity to work on and break through the patterns that continue to hold you back from manifesting your visions. This Eclipse helps us peel back one more layer of our many layered consciousnesses.

As the Moon also opposes Mercury Retrograde be cautious with your words this Eclipse. Mercury retrograde can cause miscommunication and misinterpretation. Mercury retrograde, though, does support inward communication through journalling and other methods of self-inquiry. Harness these vibrations to help you understand your shadows and how to transform them. Dig deep beneath the layers of your conscious mind to find the patterns that block your evolution. Ask yourself what you are attached to and why. Ask yourself what you are holding on to and if that energy of holding is keeping you in a frequency not aligned with your visions.

Mars adds some fire to this eclipse, reminding us to feel our passion and our ability to fight through challenging times. Mars is here to help us this day break through our shadows and face them with courage. Much of the work this eclipse asks us to do requires strength and the willingness to battle through our fears. Mars helps us face ourselves and know that we are more than capable of folding back the layers of consciousness. We may be scared of what lies beneath, but it's also better to have a map of this landscape. Mars helps us create this map on this eclipse and travel to unknown territory within ourselves.

SOUTH NODE SCOPES

The lunar eclipse is a powerful time to step away from energies governed by your South Node. Your South Node placement represents an energy that was predominant in a previous lifetime. This energy may have been your Sun sign, rising sign, or even Moon sign. You came into this life knowing this energy at the very core of your being. When it comes to your South Node, it's important to remember that it consists of the lower energies that became attached to you in a previous life. You've come into this world to find a way to shift these energies and evolve your spirit. In many ways, your South Node represents where you were misaligned in a past life. These energies always feel familiar and known to you. They form your comfort zones and may even limit your expansion.

Your South Node placement also has higher energies, but on an eclipse we are particularly looking at the lower frequencies. These energies are what form your shadow side and sabotage your greatest efforts to manifest your visions this lifetime. It's important to know that these energies are not personal. You did nothing wrong. If you find yourself embodying them, know that it's ok. Your South Node is simply part of your karmic pass this lifetime. It is your work this lifetime to find where these energies show up in your life and make efforts to shift them.

A lunar eclipse is a perfect opportunity to acknowledge these vibrations and understand them at their deepest level. As you read over your South Node description, ask yourself if it resonates with you. Then make a commitment to pay attention when these energies show up in your life. Consciously choose another path. Your South Node will always offer you the path of comfort. It's up to you to choose another road, often governed by your North Node.

Your North Node is the antidote to your South Node. It is the path away from the lower energies of your South Node and includes the lessons you are here to embrace this lifetime. If you are wondering how to detach from your South Node, look to your North Node for the answer. The North Node will feel foreign to you and even uncomfortable at first. With time, it will begin to feel like home and you will know that it is the way forward to your highest energetic evolution. Make some effort on this lunar eclipse to embrace your north nodal energies and say goodbye to those of your South Node.

SOUTH NODE SCOPES

ARIES SOUTH NODE: With your South Node in Aries, you have come into this life with a propensity for battle. This war may be against yourself or it may be against others. You most likely were a great warrior in a previous life, having to fight for what you believed. You often fought alone. You may feel at times that you are better off by yourself and that others cannot help you. You may have felt like a loner in your younger years and resisted asking people around you for support. It's important to acknowledge where you are lacking intimate connections in your life because of the South Node. Have you told yourself that you are better off alone? Do you attempt to debate or challenge others when there's no need to? Do you challenge yourself when you don't need to? Where are you fighting instead of making peace?

Over this eclipse, make an effort to embrace your North Node energies in Libra. You are here this lifetime to understand the importance of connection. You are here to learn how to rely on others for support and even knowledge. Notice where in your life you may be going at it alone when you don't need to. Challenge yourself to make a connection this eclipse. Instead of battling with yourself, make an effort to create inner peace. Know that this world is meant to be enjoyed with others and take the opportunity to experience the magic of this eclipse with another person.

TAURUS SOUTH NODE: With your South Node in Taurus, you have come into this life attached to what is comfortable. You need to feel safe and secure, and sometimes this need limits your growth. You may even find it challenging to take leaps of faith. You may also need to know all of the answers and steps of a given path before you block it. This attachment to comfort zones limits you and your potential this lifetime. You are here to learn how to rely on yourself. You will not always know the answers, but what you do know is that you will figure them out as you go. It's important to ask yourself questions when you're holding yourself back. Are you remaining in a safe position out of fear of uncertainty or because there is real danger ahead? Are you limiting your growth because it feels scary? And what can you do to ensure that you always can rely on yourself?

On the eclipse, notice how these energies show up in your life. Become keenly aware if you are limiting yourself out of fear of the unknown. Challenge yourself to take a risk or do something that feels foreign to you. Know that it may not work out, but that's ok. Sometimes the best learning occurs when things go in an unplanned direction. Trust yourself, trust your connection with nature, and trust the process of your life. Make a bold step on this eclipse to walk away from a comfort zone and into the unfamiliar, where all of your potential lies.

GEMINI SOUTH NODE: With your South Node in Gemini, you have come into this life attached to impulse. Your mind moves at a rapid speed, which in some cases can be a good thing but in others can cause you to spin in circles. You make quick decisions that incorporate things happening at the moment, but you may not see the bigger picture or long-term consequences. You may even make many mistakes that are contributed to naivete even as you grow older. You may also focus too much on the details of what you're doing, becoming immersed in the trees and forgetting to see the forest. While the details of your plans are important, so is the overarching vision you are cultivating in your life. It's also important to become aware when you are over-extending your energy instead of concentrating it where it matters most.

SOUTH NODE SCOPES

On this eclipse, make a commitment to ground your energy and dive deeper into life. This lifetime is about seeing the bigger picture and slowing down enough to focus on new horizons. It's a time for you to think more deeply and intuitively about your life by focusing on the higher meaning of your moment here. If you find yourself spinning in circles in your mind this day, slow down and ground your energy with the Earth. Spend time journaling and even reading longer passages of information that help you form a clear view about where you're ultimately headed in this life.

CANCER SOUTH NODE: With your South Node in Cancer, you have come into this world with a propensity to give. While giving can be a good thing, in your case you may find that people take advantage of you or that you allow them to get away with things that really don't serve your self-care. You may even find that people become overly dependent on you to support them, and you give them unconditional love even though they may not deserve it. You are a forgiving person and may find yourself extending liberties to people who don't extend them back. You are a person everyone relies on, but in this lifetime you need to learn how to take care of yourself first.

On this eclipse, recognize how you make other people a priority in your life over yourself. Know that your compassionate side is something to be admired, but boundaries are significant for you to learn this lifetime. With your North Node in Capricorn, it's important to place focus on your life's work and soul's journey. This lifetime is about finding and taking care of your passion. It's about nourishing yourself and knowing that when you are recharged and fulfilled, it helps others. Make a commitment on this eclipse to transform any habits that cause you to put yourself second.

LEO SOUTH NODE: With your South Node in Leo, you have come into this world trapped by the energy of royalty. You may have been a king or queen in a previous life, a leader, or somebody with high privilege. You know what it's like to be looked to for advice or even seen as a role model. This may make you feel that you need to do great things in this lifetime to the point that you feel pressure from every angle. This pressure may cause you to overly focus on gaining approval from those around you to ensure that you are getting it right. You feel you are the center of attention in every room, and this attention may not always feel good. In fact, it often makes you feel vulnerable. This vulnerability can cause you to act out, cause drama, or simply want to run away and hide.

On this eclipse, recognize that you do carry leadership energy within your vibration. Being a true leader, though, involves being who you really are and saying what you really feel even if you are rejected. Learn to approve of yourself before any member of the audience starts clapping. Also, know that what you do or say is not always for your benefit but for the benefit of the people you are leading. You're here to be a bright star, and so is everybody else. Find your own path in this lifetime and know that when you do, it encourages everybody around you to find theirs.

VIRGO SOUTH NODE: With your South Node in Virgo, you've come to this world attached to the energy of perfectionism. You may spend much of your life not feeling good enough or even feeling guilty for not doing enough. You may find yourself in an endless loop of procrastination where are you overanalyze the situation to the point that you cannot move forward. Your downfall is self-doubt and a lack of confidence in your own abilities. Even when society encourages you, you still feel you're missing something to make you perfect. It's important to realize in this lifetime, and in any lifetime, that perfection is unattainable. It is an illusion, and reaching for it only causes a delay in your life's plans. You are here to understand your power and learn that you already have the answers within you. They may not be perfect, but they are perfect for you.

On this eclipse, recognize where the lower energies of Virgo show up for you and how they sabotage your greatest efforts. Make a commitment to love yourself more and know that you are always good enough. Learn to lean on your incredible intuition and follow the path to your North Node in Pisces. You are here to understand that you are the Universe, and that in itself is perfection. Look to nature to inspire you, and see how the imperfections of everything around you make the journey of living more wonderful. Focus on what you love about yourself on this eclipse and on your infinite potential to be anything you want.

LIBRA SOUTH NODE: With your South Node in Libra, you have come into this world attached to the energy of people-pleasing. You make a great partner to everybody else, just not always to yourself. You often put other people's needs before your own and even prioritize their lives over yours. You make concessions for others that can cause resentment to build. And while you're always trying to create peace around you, at times you may find your emotions boiling over as this resentment culminates. Your work this lifetime is to learn how to balance your soul's mission and make it a priority while enjoying life with others. It's about putting yourself first and not feeling guilty for doing so.

On this eclipse, recognize where you are making choices and doing things for other people that do not serve your highest good. Notice how you are blocking your own evolution and growth by making your partners the priority. Also, notice if you are putting more importance on their life's mission and work over your own. Challenge yourself to transform these habits and, instead of making the people around you a priority, make yourself number one. On the eclipse, do something selfish for yourself and take back any power that you have given to others that rightly belongs to you.

SCORPIO SOUTH NODE: With your South Node in Scorpio, you have come into this world understanding the complexities of life. Your previous life may have been full of hardships that taught you many lessons through events most people would not want to encounter. You have a unique psychological depth and carry significant wisdom within you. You may even be called an old soul, for your eyes speak of the many lifetimes you've lived on this planet. Your natural pull is toward the complexities of life, including your own mind. You may look for hidden agendas and ulterior motives everywhere. You may even mistrust the people around you, always suspecting that there's something more at play. This lifetime is governed by your North Node in Taurus, which teaches you to rely on the Earth and trust the support it gives you. It's about feeling at peace within your energy and calming down from the journey you have undertaken to land here.

On this eclipse, you are in alignment with the current lunar nodes. This is an amazing opportunity for you to let go of some of the lower frequencies of Scorpio and embrace the higher energies of Taurus. The next year is a powerful period of transformation for you, when you can release shadows from a previous time and shift them into finding the light within you. It's a time for you to slow down, trust

SOUTH NODE SCOPES

the ground beneath you, and find some peace within your soul. It's also time for you to enjoy the simple pleasures of life and know that you do not always have to be looking for the deeper meaning everywhere. Yes, life is complex, but it contains pure moments of simple beauty. Set aside your need to overanalyze things and instead enjoy what's on the surface.

SAGITTARIUS SOUTH NODE: With your South Node in Sagittarius, you have come into this world with broad horizons. You have spent much time traveling foreign lands and have experienced different cultures much more than other people. You may have found yourself in the trap of assuming you knew all there was to know in the world. You may have even stopped learning at some point because you felt you had already seen it all. There's also a tendency with the South Node in Sagittarius to subscribe to dogmatic thinking. You may have learned many philosophies, and even religious beliefs, and then settled into one. This commitment to one perspective caused you to close yourself off from different viewpoints, assuming that you already ruled them out as incorrect. In closing your perspective, you missed the higher meaning of universal energy, which teaches that everything is connected. With your North Node in Gemini, this lifetime is about becoming amazed and even entranced by life itself. This lifetime is about learning new perspectives, seeing the world through fresh eyes, and becoming an everlasting student of life.

On this eclipse, notice where you are assuming that you already know the answer. Become aware of how you have shut yourself off from different perspectives and ask yourself why. Instead, open yourself to novel information that teaches you about new energies in the world. Be curious and, in that curiosity, find a fresh outlook on life. You do not need to know everything there is to know in this world. You just need to ask questions. When you don't receive answers in alignment with your beliefs, ask yourself how you can open your mind to incorporate all the energies the Universe has to offer.

CAPRICORN SOUTH NODE: With your South Node in Capricorn, you have come into this world with focus and determination. In a previous lifetime, you endured hardships that caused you to exist in survival mode. You innately understand some of the crueler energies of life, like famine, long cold winters, and poverty. Because of this, you learned to not rely upon anybody but yourself. It is not in your nature to ask for help, and it is challenging for you to receive it. You carry a certain strength about you. With this gift also comes a seriousness that does not allow you to explore your emotions or fully enjoy the gifts of this life. The antidote to these South Node energies is your North Node in Cancer. This lifetime is about allowing yourself to be held. It's about crying when you need to cry and nourishing yourself with the comfort of care. It's about softening and knowing that you don't always have to travel the road alone. You can ask for help, and there will be people for you to rely upon. There will also be people to enjoy life and have heart-expanding experiences with if you allow yourself to open.

On the eclipse, let yourself feel. Notice where you're holding back your emotions underneath a hard shell and give yourself permission to crack open. Ask for help if you need it and, more importantly, allow yourself to receive it. Recognize your strength but also recognize where you can take down some of the walls that guard your heart. Let people in and let them surprise you. Let yourself be loved and nourished, knowing that you are cared for in this world.

SOUTH NODE SCOPES

AQUARIUS SOUTH NODE: With your South Node in Aquarius, you have come into this world carrying an immense amount of knowledge. You have spent previous lifetimes observing behaviors of society and understanding them on a fundamental level. These progressive ideas led you to become at odds with societal norms and customs. Even though you saw how other people around you needed to evolve in their ideas, they were not ready to understand you. This lack of understanding led you to feel like an outsider, and you may have been labeled the rebel. You may have even been exiled at one point or exiled yourself. With your South Node in Aquarius, you may have seen the path forward for society but chose to disconnect yourself from others and focus on your individual growth instead of the collective's. This lifetime is governed by the energy of Leo, encouraging you to step into the spotlight and become a leader. This journey is about taking your innate knowledge of society and stepping into a visionary role that allows you to share these beliefs and evolve the collective forward.

On the eclipse, notice if any leftover energies from the South Node in Aquarius are showing up in your life. Are you disconnecting from society or the collective in some way? Are you withholding your knowledge for fear that you will be misunderstood? Do you feel you don't quite belong and therefore try to fit in even though it goes against your natural constitution? Ask yourself how you become a leader and use your ideas to help move society toward a brighter future. Instead of dissociating from the collective, make a commitment to become a leader and stand in the spotlight that is waiting for you.

PISCES SOUTH NODE: With your South Node in Pisces, you come into this world understanding a vast amount of knowledge and the interconnectedness of energy that threads the Universe together. In a previous lifetime, you most likely devoted yourself to varying paths of spirituality. You understand how the Universe works on a fundamental level and have completed your education in life itself. When you hear of different energetic modalities, religions, and spiritual paths, you do not feel like you are learning them for the first time but are remembering them. This is knowledge you already hold within your vibration. This lifetime is not about escaping into different realms of consciousness that teach you about the Universe. It's about taking what you already know, grounding it, and giving it to others in an organized fashion. You are a teacher this life. You may at first feel overwhelmed by the responsibility placed upon you or think you are lacking in some way and need to learn more. These feelings may cause you to do things that distract you from your life's path. It's important for you to continually align with your North Node in Virgo and make an effort to be a mentor to those around you. You are here this lifetime to serve and explain the mysteries of the Universe to the collective.

On this eclipse, become aware of ways that you distract yourself or escape into different realms of consciousness. How do you avoid your life's path as a teacher and instead fall back into your comfort zone of a student? How do you get lost in energetics portals of discovery instead of bringing the knowledge down to Earth and giving it to people in a way that they can understand? Throughout this eclipse, shed any fear you have about your imperfections and acknowledge that you already know enough. You are ready to teach and lead others. Feel your intuition guiding you to take some steps that bring your knowledge into a tangible format that can be received by others.

SCORPIO LUNAR FLOW

Scorpio rules the hips and pelvis, the seat of our creativity. This energy is ruled by water, making it fluid. Scorpio reminds us to move our bodies with ease and grace. Through the soft opening of the body, we can move stagnant energy and release blocks against our own evolution. This sequence is designed to put you in touch with the natural rhythm of your energy and encourage it to flow evenly through your whole being.

THREAD-THE-NEEDLE POSE

Begin with your back on your mat. Bend both knees and cross your left ankle over your right knee, making a four with your legs. Thread your left arm through the hole of the four and grasp your right hand around your right shin, picking up that leg. Make sure your neck is relaxed; use a pillow under your head if needed. Breathe here for 5 deep breaths, sending each inhale down into your hips and releasing the tension on the exhale. Then switch sides.

SEATED SEQUENCE

Come up to a cross-legged position. With your spine upright, make circles in your hips, rolling your torso around. Continue this for about 30 seconds, then switch directions. Feel the fluid movement of your body.

Come back to center and interlace your hands behind your head. On inhale, twist to the right. Exhale, twist to the left. Do this for 1 minute, then release.

Still seated, place your hands on your knees, then arch and round your back. Feel the full undulation of your spine as it waves back and forth. Even feel your neck and throat open as you arch your spine. Continue for 1 minute, then return to stillness.

CAT/COW TO DOWNWARD-FACING DOG

Come onto your hands and knees. Arch your back on inhale, then round it on exhale. Again, feel the wave of your spine and the fluidity of your movement. Continue for 1 minute. Come back to center and roll through your rib cage, making large circles with your torso. Continue for 30 seconds before switching sides. There is no right or wrong way to do these; just move organically and in tune with your body. Come back to center and exhale into Downward Dog.

SCORPIO LUNAR FLOW

SUN SALUTATION A - 5 ROUNDS

Stand at the top of your mat. Inhale, stretch your arms overhead > Exhale, fold forward > Inhale, lengthen out your back > Exhale, step back to Plank Pose and lower > Inhale, reach your chest up for Cobra Pose, legs on the ground > Exhale, Downward Dog. Stay here for 5 breaths and feel your entire body expand. On Exhale, step to the top of your mat > Inhale, lengthen through your spine > Exhale, fold forward > Inhale, come up to standing, reaching arms overhead > Exhale, hands to your heart. Pause for a moment and feel yourself centered throughout your body.

On your fifth round, remain in Downward Dog and breathe for 5 breaths.

LUNGE > WARRIOR 2 > GODDESS POSE

From Downward Dog, step your left foot forward into a Lunge Pose. Your back heel will lift from the ground and your leg will stay straight. Bend deeply into your front knee as you tilt your tailbone toward the ground. Reach your arms to the sky and send your breath into your hips. After 5 breaths, open up into Warrior 2. Spin your back foot flat inward on the ground at a 45-degree angle and rotate your torso to the right side of your mat, reaching your arms to either side. Bend in your front knee, pressing it out to the left. Take 5 breaths here, opening up your pelvis and grounding down through your legs. Inhale, straighten your leg, and bring your feet to parallel in a wide-legged stance. Turn your toes out to a 45-degree angle and bend in your knees for Goddess Pose. Bend your arms by your sides with your palms facing the sky. Breathe here for 5 breaths as you feel your feet root into the ground. Once complete, straighten your legs and rotate your right foot out, repeating Warrior 2 and Lunge on this side. From Warrior 2, release your hands to the ground and step back through a Vinyasa or straight to Downward Dog.

MALASANA (SQUAT POSE)

Hop your feet forward to the outside of your hands with your feet hips width or wider and your toes slightly turned out. Drop your hips down for a Squat Pose. Press firmly through the outer edges of your feet and feel your heels energetically draw together. If your heels lift from the ground, place a blanket beneath them or sit on a block until your hips release and open. Take 5 deep breaths here, allowing your hips to open as your feet root into the Earth. Release into a forward bend, hanging over your legs as your spine releases.

PIGEON POSE

Return to Downward Dog through a Vinyasa or by stepping back and taking your left knee to your left wrist for Pigeon Pose. Go easy on your knee. If you feel any pain, return to Thread the Needle. Carefully lay down your left leg and stretch your right leg back. Before folding, press up through your hands and arch your back a bit, stretching through the front of your body. On exhale, fold forward over your leg and remain here for 10 breaths. On each inhale, send your breath into your hips, encouraging them to open. On exhale, release a bit more. After 10 breaths, slowly switch sides.

SAVASANA

Release to the floor, lying with your palms up and your eyes closed. Feel your body alive with fresh energy circulating throughout your system. Feel the ground beneath you supporting you. Know this support is always available to you from Mother Earth. Rest here fully for 5 minutes.

18

LUNAR ECLIPSE MEDITATION

KAPALABHATI PRANAYAMA

Focusing and altering our breath is one of the tools of alchemy we possess. Breathwork is relatively easy and can be done anywhere. Kapalabhati, or breath of fire, is an ancient yogic breathwork that helps purify the energetic body. It also brings in new, fresh energy to be worked with and circulated throughout your body. Practice this breathwork on the days surrounding the Full Moon to help process and digest all the information the New Moon brings to you. This breathwork will also transmute feelings of heaviness into lightness, giving you the perfect tool when your breath becomes stagnant or the energy around you feels too intense.

Sit in a comfortable position with your spine straight. You can sit on a cushion or pillow to elevate your hips higher than your knees. Relax your shoulders, but feel your core supporting your spine. Close your eyes and take a deep inhale, then exhale. On your next inhale, fill up only two-thirds of the way with air. On the exhale, release short, sharp exhales out through your nose, pumping your belly. It will feel like you are attempting to blow out a candle with your nose on the exhale. Focus solely on your exhales, allowing the inhales to come naturally. Continue this for 50 rounds of exhales. Afterward, take a deep inhale and hold your breath for a count of 10. Exhale slowly. Repeat the entire sequence for a second time. Once you finish both sets, allow your breath to become natural. Feel into the expansion you've created and observe the feeling of new energy circulating throughout your system.

GOLDEN LIGHT ALIGNMENT MEDITATION

Come into a comfortable seated position with your spine upright. Allow your shoulders and neck to relax. Feel rooted down through your pelvis. Imagine a golden sun above your head, raining down the light of unconditional love upon you. Breathe in this warm, golden light through the crown of your head and your third eye. Feel this light warm the inside of your head, opening your vision and anchoring you in the present. Feel the light down to your throat, opening and aligning your throat chakra as you learn to speak your truth. Radiate this light down into your heart, feeling it expand and fill your rib cage. Send this light into your lungs, filling them with white, golden light and opening up your body's ability to heal itself. Circulate this light down into your solar plexus, the seat of your willpower. Feel it open your center of power here as it calls in your courage. Send the light down to your navel to your sacral chakra, the seat of your creativity. Allow it to open this area, encouraging you to feel your intuition and your instinctual knowledge. Continue sending the light down through your torso into your root chakra, the base of your pelvis. Feel it anchoring you to the present and allowing you to feel safe, supported, and grounded here. Feel this entire beam of light raining down through your crown chakra to the base of your pelvis, lighting you up from the inside out and aligning you with the power of the Sun—the same power you hold inside you.

ECLIPSE CIRCLE SET UP

The Scorpio lunar eclipse begins at 8:14 am. Pacific time. It reaches its maximum eclipse at 10:22 a.m. Pacific time and concludes at 12:31 p.m. Pacific time. If possible, hold your eclipse ritual and practice during this time. You can even set up your space outside to feel its energy more fully. If you cannot practice in this time frame, complete your rituals twenty-four hours before or after the eclipse, when the energy is still potent.

To set up your circle for this eclipse, choose a space that feels safe, protected, and grounded. The energy of the eclipse can cause us to feel restless or insecure in our bodies. It's important to harness the elements of nature to ground your energy and help you feel connected through the eclipse. Create a circle anchored with objects, like crystals and candles. Incorporate all the elements, including Water for Scorpio and Earth for Taurus. For Air, incorporate auric sprays, feathers to fan smoke, and even wind chimes to hear the air moving around you. Choose candles to represent

ECLIPSE CIRCLE SET UP

Fire or build an outside fire. You can use crystals to represent the Earth element. Crystals that align with Scorpio's energy are Smokey Quartz, Hematite, Black Tourmaline, Shungite, and Obsidian. These crystals will help rid you of negative frequencies and protect your energy from vibrations others may be shedding. Also, include some crystals to represent Taurus—such as Jade, Pink Opal, Topaz, Green Onyx, and Kyanite—as this energy is very much involved tonight. These crystals will help ground your energy and keep you connected to your body and nature. Bring in the Water element through a room diffuser, a vase with flowers in it, or just a simple silver metal bowl containing water. If you are located near an ocean or river, try to set up your circle there to bring in the Water element. Gather all of your supplies and build your circle.

Create an outline with your objects, anchoring the four directions—north, south, east, and west—with either a crystal or candle. If you are creating an altar, set it up in the westerly part of the circle, as this direction gives way for the release of energies. Once the perimeter is set, cleanse the area with a dried herb or an auric spray. Rosemary is an excellent herb to cleanse yourself and your space. It provides cleansing, clarity, and protection. Use some dried rosemary in a smudge stick, or you can place some in a metal bowl to burn. Begin cleansing at the easterly point, moving to the south, west, and north, then back to the east. Imagine a white light encasing the circle, protecting it from any external energies. Light your candles, and place the rest of your crystals in the circle.

Once your perimeter is set, fill it in by placing larger crystals or a crystal grid in the center to anchor your circle. If creating a crystal grid, use a spiral formation with a sphere in the middle for the Water element—the night's dominant element. Before your guests enter, cleanse each one of them and then cleanse yourself. Once you have all entered the circle, pause for a moment to let the energy settle before you begin. If you are leading others, sit in the northern position of the circle, which holds the seat of knowledge. Also, have some crystals near you, like Aquamarine or Chrysocolla, to aid in communication. Also have some that let you feel your intuition and knowledge, like Lemurian or Moonstone. Your guests can fill in around you.

You can practice alone or in a group. Scorpio's energy tends to cause inward reflection on the deepest level and may lead you to practice alone. You do not need others for a Moon circle, you need only yourself and your willingness to connect with nature. Follow your intuitive guidance when leading a circle for yourself or others. If you are with others, open the circle by having everyone introduce themselves. Review and meditate on the energy of the night brought to us by both the eclipse and Scorpio. Feel into the interaction between the Sun in Taurus and the Moon in Scorpio, which you are sitting among. If you feel called to, move your body through yoga and then settle your energy through meditation. Then dive into the practices in this workbook. Give yourself plenty of time and space to learn from them. Allow the answers to reveal themselves. Share as much, or as little, as you want with the people you may be with, and then end the night with a releasing ritual to honor the releasing power of this eclipse.

Conclude the circle by giving gratitude to yourself, the room, the planet, and the Universe for supporting you and helping you transform into your best, most powerful self.

SCORPIO ECLIPSE PRACTICES

Lunar eclipses are powerful times for release and renewal. If possible, practice this releasing ritual during the eclipse window and feel these energies detach from your field and enter another space. You can focus on lower energies of Scorpio or energies from your South Node placement. This eclipse is your opportunity to say goodbye to stagnant energies that have been stuck with you for years and maybe even lifetimes. Feel the power of this eclipse and harness it to clear the way to higher visions.

After you've completed the practices in this workbook:

1. Take out three pieces of paper.

2. On one, write what you are retleasing this eclipse and give permission to the waters of Scorpio to wash it away.

3. On the second, write what intention or seed you are planting into the fertile and abundant earth of Taurus.

4. On the third, write what you are grateful for tonight.

5. Gather the releasing notes and burn them (safely) in a cauldron.

6. If possible, gather some of the ashes and put them in a bowl of water with clear Quartz. Leave this bowl outside all night under the Full Moon once the eclipse has ended to further cleanse the energies.

7. Gather the intention notes and place them under a crystal—like Quartz, Citrine, Lemurian, or Jade—in the most easterly corner of your home. Leave them there for a week, then put them away in a notebook. You can create an altar here of crystals, poems or words that inspire you, affirmations, and images of people who have guided or continue to guide you.

8. For the gratitude notes, pass them to the person on the left, and then everyone will take their neighbor's home. If you are practicing alone, place your gratitude note somewhere you can see it to remind yourself every day of your abundance.

_____

_____

_____

_____

_____

_____

_____

_____

SCORPIO PRACTICES

The Scorpio lunar eclipse is a perfect time to dive into your shadows and do some shadow work. Shadow work was originally explained and conceived by Carl Jung, a psychiatrist in the early to mid-1900s. He talked about the shadow being a core part of the personality and one we need to understand to understand ourselves. Simply put, we're all born with seeds of potential, but not all of these potentials are nourished. These seeds represent energetic patterns that are universal, meaning everyone has them. Jung explained them as universal archetypes, or patterns of energy, that are shared by the collective unconscious. He talked of twelve main archetypes. These patterns of energy can also correlate with the twelve zodiac signs. We all are connected to every archetypal energy in the Universe, but only some of them become predominant in our personality. The lower sides of these energies, whether we are talking about Jungian archetypes or zodiac archetypes, become our shadows.

We are all born with the energetic seeds of potential, and through our upbringing, we are taught to nourish some seeds and bring them to full bloom. We are also taught to suppress, deny, or reject other seeds. Those parts of ourselves that our caregivers and society teach us to repress become our shadow. Our shadow is neither good nor bad. We often think of the shadow as our demons or monsters, but it's really just energies that we were taught to repress or ignore, so we actively cut ourselves off from these parts of ourselves and deny their existence.

We create shadows for many reasons. For instance, if we couldn't process an emotion at the time it occurred, it ended up in our shadow. Or if we are taught that if we felt a certain way, we would lose the love of our caregivers, that emotion ends up in the shadow. What ended up in our shadow is just out of our view. We can't see it, but it does control us. For instance, if a child becomes angry at their caregiver and that caregiver withdraws love and attention or, worse, punishes the child, the child learns to never be angry. They pack their anger away and deny it. Years may go by and this person may think they never get angry, but in reality, that anger is controlling them unconsciously. It's affecting their life and will continue to do so until they face it and accept that they have anger and may even be angry.

Shadow work is about accepting what is in your shadows. It's about integrating those lost emotions and behaviors, and owning them. Once that child who suppressed their anger owns it, they can own their life. When we bring what is in the shadows to the light, it loses its power. Shadow work is not about releasing and getting rid of what is in the shadow—it's about acceptance. When we accept the shadows, we can understand and channel them. They can help us instead of hinder us.

In accepting our shadows, we accept that there is nothing wrong with our anger, anxiety, or sadness. We don't have to ignore it or get rid of it. We only need to own it. Shadow work is about accepting all energies within us with love and compassion.

SCORPIO PRACTICES

Once we own our shadows, we own our life. We are empowered to be who we want to be. We are able to make conscious decisions that put us in control of our life, grounded in the truth. The joy and gift of shadow work is that we become the true creators of our life. We no longer are controlled by unconscious emotions set out to sabotage us or keep us in comfort zones. We become free to live our without fear, without worrying about what others think, and with a complete understanding of who we are and what we need. We become radically honest with ourselves and radically accepting.

Shadows are tricky, though, since they are just out of view. They can be challenging to identify. On this eclipse, allow the light of the Moon to help you find them and transmute them. One of the easiest ways to find your shadows is to notice when you are triggered. When you are triggered, you react emotionally, but not in a way that is a match for the situation. You overreact or even have a reaction that doesn't feel like yourself. It's as if someone has taken over your mind and body and you have lost control. This exaggerated reaction is your first clue that your shadow has been triggered. And oftentimes it is another person who is triggering you. And you, in turn, project your shadow onto them. For instance, if a person packed their anger away in their shadow, they may become triggered by people who are angry. They may have an intense reaction to someone who is angry or frustrated, even if that anger is not directed to them. They may respond in various ways to anger, but their responses do not feel like them. Those responses are misplaced for the situation at hand. Conversely, this person may also project anger onto others. So if they are in a relationship, they may often accuse their partner of being angry when they, in fact, are the one who is angry—not their partner.

Through self-inquiry and examination, you can see ways in which you overreact to situations or people and ways you may project your shadow onto others. The people in your life serve as mirrors for your shadow. The ones who trigger you the most are the ones you have the most to learn from. It can be challenging to accept that the person who annoys you or who you can't possibly understand is the key to unlocking your freedom, but this is how shadow work is done. You must be willing to become uncomfortable to free yourself of your shadows.

As you move through life this eclipse, notice who triggers you. Ask yourself why they trigger you and if your reaction is warranted or if it is your shadow talking. Is the person triggering you really reflecting an unconscious part of yourself? Are they casting light on your shadow and making you uncomfortable with the revelation of your true self?

Likewise, look at how you may be projecting your shadow onto other people, especially your close relationships. Your shadows will try to rope others into playing roles or control dramas from your childhood. Your shadows want to be indulged. They are manipulative and will try to manipulate people to play a role that feeds them. You may also simply put your emotions onto others as a way to deflect them from yourself. Notice when you assume you know how someone is feeling and instead, ask yourself if it is you who feels this way.

The most important part of shadow work is to remember it is rooted in love. It's about loving and accepting all sides of yourself. In this acceptance, you will find freedom. Shadow work is not about picking yourself apart. It's about acknowledging every aspect of yourself with compassion until you feel whole.

SCORPIO PRACTICES

1. What situation or person has triggered an emotional response from you in the past week? How does this make your heart feel?

_____

_____

_____

_____

_____

_____

_____

_____

_____

_____

_____

_____

_____

_____

_____

_____

_____

_____

_____

_____

_____

_____

_____

SCORPIO PRACTICES

2. What is something about your childhood that made you feel you couldn't act a certain way or that an emotion wasn't accepted? What happened to that behavior or emotion? How is it asking to be seen and accepted today?

_____

_____

_____

_____

_____

_____

_____

_____

_____

_____

_____

_____

_____

_____

_____

_____

_____

_____

_____

_____

_____

_____

_____

_____

SCORPIO PRACTICES

$3.$ Who are your mirrors? And what can you learn from them?

_____

_____

_____

_____

_____

_____

_____

_____

_____

_____

_____

_____

_____

$4.$ What are some of your common projections onto others? What do they tell you about your shadows?

_____

_____

_____

_____

_____

_____

_____

_____

_____

_____

_____

_____

SCORPIO PRACTICES

_____

_____

_____

_____

_____

_____

_____

5. What patterns appear in your communications with others and yourself that are clues to your triggers and emotional shadows? How is your unconscious directing the conversation, and how can you break free of this control?

_____

_____

_____

_____

_____

_____

_____

_____

_____

_____

_____

_____

_____

_____

_____

_____

_____

_____

SCORPIO PRACTICES

6. Are there any repeating situations, people, or patterns that cause you pain and suffering? What do these recurring themes reveal about your shadows?

_____

_____

_____

_____

_____

_____

_____

_____

_____

_____

_____

_____

_____

7. What outdated behavior once served you but is no longer part of who you are or what you need?

_____

_____

_____

_____

_____

_____

_____

_____

_____

SCORPIO PRACTICES

_____

_____

_____

_____

_____

_____

_____

_____

_____

8. What deeper emotion may be hiding behind the one you are feeling when triggered? What shadow are you denying that is ready to break through to your conscious mind?

_____

_____

_____

_____

_____

_____

_____

_____

_____

_____

_____

_____

_____

_____

_____

SCORPIO PRACTICES

9. How does it feel to observe your triggers rather than react to them?
What are you learning about yourself through this observation?

SCORPIO PRACTICES

10. Who are you without your shadows? How have your shadows made life feel predictable? How can you remind yourself that it's ok to feel uncomfortable in the unknown without them?

_____

_____

_____

_____

_____

_____

_____

_____

_____

_____

_____

_____

_____

_____

_____

_____

_____

_____

_____

_____

_____

_____

_____

_____

_____

_____

_____

AFFIRMATIONS

Make a list of how you can continue to connect with your light and intuition. Know this is the path to overcoming your shadows. What opens your heart and allows you to hear your intuition? What does your intuition sound like when you are operating from your shadows? What does your intuition tell you about your healing?

HAPPY
FULL MOON!

Thank you to everyone who supported and purchased this workbook.

Special Thanks to Rebecca Reitz (rebeccareitz.com, @becca_reitz) for her beautiful artwork on the cover, page 4, 10, 18.

For a monthly subscription contact hello@spiritdaughter.com or visit www.spiritdaughter.com.

Disclaimer: The exercises and yoga sequences in this book are physical activities that should be performed carefully to avoid injury. You agree to accept all risks and release Spirit Daughter and any guest instructors from any and all liabilities. Please take care and enjoy.

Follow along our journey on IG:
@spiritdaughter

We always love seeing your photos & hearing about your experiences with the workbooks! Tag us to be featured on our community page:
@spiritdaughtercollective